A
AND A YANK
OF HAIR

Johnny Hart

FAWCETT GOLD MEDAL · NEW YORK

Library of Congress Catalog Card Number: 84-91716

ISBN 0-449-12650-1

Manufactured in the United States of America

First Ballantine Books Edition: March 1985

10 9 8 7 6 5 4 3 2 1

6-19

6-21

BONG

WHAT IN THE
WORLD
WAS THAT?

...MY NEW JAPANESE
GRANDFATHER'S CLOCK.

7·1

hart

7.3

7.4

stere·o·type

WILEY'S DICTIONARY

a siamese secretary

WILEY'S DICTIONARY

7-11

AAAAHHHHHH

7-12

IF YOU GOT AN ITCH....
SCRATCH IT.

7.15

7-29

8.3

8-4

8.5

8·10

8·11

HUNKY·Dory

8·15

an obese boat

WILEY'S DICTIONARY

hur·ly-bur·ly

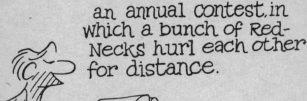

an annual contest, in which a bunch of Red-Necks hurl each other for distance.

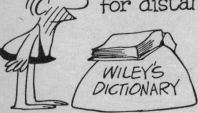

WILEY'S DICTIONARY

8·16

hart

skeleton: key *n.*

8·17

a device for opening closet doors

sun·dial *n.*

WILEY'S
DICTIONARY

8·18

a thermostat
for solar homes

WILEY'S
DICTIONARY

hart

middle·ear

8·19

an eavesdropper

8-28

SAUFFLE
SHUFFLE

9-5

MEOOOW

WHAM

EVIDENTLY,.... SHE'S NOT TOO
FOND OF CATS EITHER.

LOOK SEE, SEE DICK
AND JANE.

9·11

SEE THEM HAVE FUN
ON THE BEACH.

SEE DICK GIVE
ANOTHER GIRL
THE EYE

SEE THE NURSE GIVE
DICK THE EYE.

OH LOOK, SEE SPOT
CHASE PUFF

SEE PUFF RUN UP
THE TREE

9-12

SEE SPOT RUN UP
THE TREE

HEAR THE FIRE
DEPARTMENT TELL
DICK WHERE TO GO.

LOOK, LOOK, SEE SPOT BARE HIS TEETH AT PUFF

OH LOOK, SEE PUFF BARE HER CLAWS.

SEE SPOT BARK AT PUFF

SEE PUFF REMOVE SPOT'S SPOT.

OH LOOK, SEE JANE

9.15

SEE HER BAKE A CRABAPPLE PIE

SEE DICK WOLF DOWN JANE'S PIE

SEE THE LIGHT BURN ALL NIGHT IN DICK'S BATHROOM.

SEE DICK GIVE JANE A FLOWER

9-16

SEE JANE PLUCK THE PETALS AND SAY, "HE LOVES ME, HE LOVES ME NOT."

SEE JANE DECK DICK.

9.27

10·4

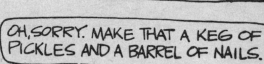

10.10

10-11

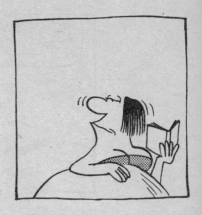

hart

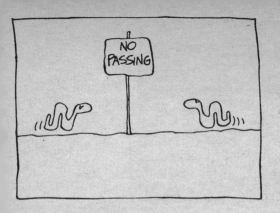

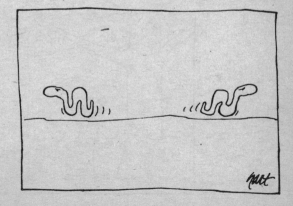

KLUNK

10.17

SAW'RIGHT.

..'YOU LIKE ?

S'NICE

SLAM

Hart

10·18

10-19

10.23

10·24

ZIP

10-8

11-1

11-4

11·10

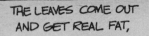

11·17

11·24

funny·bone

definitely not a "ha-ha" part of your anatomy

11-27

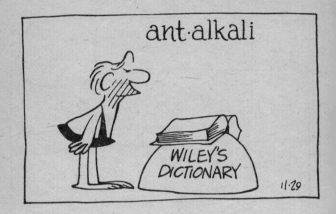

ant·alkali

WILEY'S DICTIONARY

11·29

Uncle Seltzer's wife.

WILEY'S DICTIONARY

hart

SQUIRRELS PICK UP LOTS OF NUTS AND STORE THEM IN THEIR CHEEKS,

12·2

AND PELICANS CAN TAKE THOSE FISH AND STORE 'EM IN THEIR BEAKS,

AND SNAKES OF SIZE WITH GREAT BIG EYES CAN EAT A PIG OR TWO,

BUT I WOULD HAVE TO FAST FOR WEEKS TO FEAST MY EYES ON YOU.

124

129

ABOUT THE AUTHOR

As far back as he can remember, Johnny Hart ha
been drawing funny pictures, which have gotten hir
into or out of trouble, depending on the circun
stances. It wasn't until he was nineteen and m
young cartoonist Brant Parker, however, that h
seriously began to consider cartooning as
profession. In the years that followed, that ambitic
grew—nurtured by Hart's wife, Bobby, who stood k
him as he labored over kitchen tables far into th
night, hoping to join the fraternity of cartoonists h
idolized.

In 1959, his dream came true when B.C. ra
nationally for the first time. THE WIZARD OF I
followed five years later, co-created by Brant Parke
Hart has gone on to win many major awards for h
cartoons, including the prestigious Reuben Awar
for Cartoonist of the Year, in 1968. He and his wi
live in upstate New York.

An interesting sidelight to this whole saga, Hart tel
us, is that many of the characters in his strips a
patterned after true, real-life friends.

That wasn't too smart.